whispers
OF THE
HEART

30 day devotional journal

ANNE WATSON

Published by Lion Publishing
Tyler, Texas
Book design copyright ©2023
Cover photo by Carolyn V of Sixteen Miles Out - www.sixteenmilesout.com
Cover design by Sarah O'Neal - www.evecustomartwork.com
Interior design by Kristi VanDuker

ACKNOWLEDGEMENTS

Always first and foremost, my heart sings praises to my God whose living word transforms lives. The One who whispers His profound truths through my pen. I am privileged to work alongside the amazing team members He has provided to bring excellence to the finished book and glory to His name.

Beta readers Alisha Geyer, Shelley Moore and Sue Cunningham, your gracious thoughts, suggestions and comments helped immensely to begin this journey, giving Whispers of the Heart the touches that readers desire from a 30 day devotional journal.

The cover photo, with the elements staged by photographer Carolyn Watson* offers a lovely visual of the purpose of this book. Sarah O'Neal** while in the process of designing the Whispers cover, also transformed the photo into a beautiful watercolor image.

Abounding appreciation goes to Kristi VanDuker and Cheryl Giddings for our weekly brain-storming and prayer sessions. Kristi, who wears many hats; interior designer, proficient editor, typesetter, et al., tenaciously read through each page to discover any final edits. Cheryl Giddings, financial virtuoso and keeper of fiscal records, thank you for taking time to read aloud with me every devotion to capture any discrepancies.

If I have forgotten to name anyone who added in making Whispers of the Heart the God-honoring book it has become, please forgive me. My gratitude runs deep to all who have been a part of making this book a reality.

Last but definitely never least, you, my readers who bought Whispers of the Heart, thank you for taking the step to share the whispers of your heart with the Creator of the universe.

*To view Carolyn's beautiful photos go to the website below:
www.sixteenmilesout.com
**To view Sarah's amazing design work go to the website below:
www.evecustomartwork.com

ALWAYS FOR THE KING

Note to Reader

2 Peter 1:2-3
Grace and peace be multiplied to you in the knowledge of
God and of Jesus our Lord; seeing that His divine power
has granted to us everything pertaining to life and godliness,
through the true knowledge of Him who called us by His own
glory and excellence.

Are you ready to share your most intimate heart-thoughts with God? Maybe things from your past you have intentionally hidden to protect yourself from shame, guilt, pain; and/or things you chose long ago to tuck away and never revisit. Perhaps now is the time to surrender the key to your past and allow God to unveil the value of you. After all, God created you to have remarkable significance. A fresh start is reality when you unlock your heart and experience God's love.

It is said a red geranium symbolizes friendship, happiness and good health. The miracle of a blossoming flower happens in the present. Sometimes right before your eyes. Sadly, it's possible in your desire to accomplish the next thing, you rarely take time to enjoy the beauty of a flower, encourage friendships, make new acquaintances, sit with those experiencing unbearable grief or listen to the lonely. Give yourself permission to stop all the busy-ness and give someone a red geranium. Better yet, give them the gift of time. Your time. Your undivided attention and a willing heart to listen to their present circumstances is priceless.

How many times have you looked through a windowpane at the azure blue sky wondering what lies beyond? Do you gaze through that window imagining what the future might bring? When God plants a dream within you, He prepares you for what is to come. When you share the whispers of your heart with God, He graciously listens, teaching you to stop, breathe deep and listen for what He desires to share with you. Your future is secure when you trust your life to Almighty God.

I would love to hear how your 30 day commitment to daily time alone with God is transforming your life.

Abundant blessings,
Anne
watsononline1711@gmail.com

AUTHENTICITY OR FACADE

PART ONE

Colossians 2:8
*See to it that no one takes you captive through philosophy and
empty deception, according to the tradition of men, according
to the elementary principles of the world, rather than according to Christ.*

I awoke this morning from a dream about confronting people that I thought 'I
knew'. Their behavior was contrary to the godly image they presented to the
world.

The dream left me disillusioned. Surprised. Shocked. Misled. Deceived. I
asked God to show me what is behind these façades? Why can't people be
honest and authentic? Why must they put on false personas?

Then I went looking in the Bible for examples of people who were authentic
versus those who were deceptive. Not surprisingly there are many. The apostle Paul spoke of both.

Yet the characters that drew my attention are in the book of Esther. Ten brief
chapters packed with intrigue, valor, façade and authenticity.

This digging deep and retrieving information from Esther could go on for
some time.

JOURNAL

How would you define authenticity?

_____
_____
_____
_____
_____

What does the word facade bring to mind?

_____
_____
_____
_____
_____

What is your heart whispering?

_____
_____
_____
_____
_____
_____
_____
_____
_____
_____
_____
_____
_____
_____
_____
_____
_____
_____
_____
_____
_____
_____

AUTHENTICITY OR FACADE
PART TWO

Esther 2:17
The king loved Esther more than all the women, and she
found favor and kindness with him more than all the virgins,
so that he set the royal crown on her head and made her
queen instead of Vashti.

The book of Esther is fascinating. We will find several authentic and deceptive examples throughout the book. We could dissect it chapter by chapter,
even verse by verse and discover the who, what, when, where, how and why
of this historical book. But keeping with the original question of whether the
people in this story are living their lives with authenticity or behind a façade,
we will look mainly at the characters in the book.

Esther begins with royalty: King Ahasuerus, his wife Queen Vashti, and an
insurrection. Vashti strikes me as rather arrogant. She definitely lands on
the façade side of the question. One has to wonder if the queen might have
played a compliant role up until this point and finally decided to take a rather
rebellious stand refusing to be paraded in front of the king's guests.

King Ahasuerus seems bent on making sure everyone sees his royal glory
and the splendor of his great majesty by displaying his riches for six months,
as well as showing off the beauty of his queen. At this point in the story, his
character is shown by the façade of his kingly station and his vast wealth.

When Vashti challenges the king's authority, he bans her from the throne
and searches for another to take her place. Hadassah, a Jewish orphan (who
is now named Esther and is cared for by her cousin Mordecai), won favor
and was chosen to be the next queen. Due to her authenticity and innocence
Esther finds favor with the king and with everyone else who knows her.

JOURNAL

Who are the people in your life who live behind a façade?

_____
_____
_____
_____
_____

Who are the people in your life who are authentic?

_____
_____
_____
_____
_____

How do you know who they really are?

_____
_____
_____
_____
_____

What is your heart whispering?

_____
_____
_____
_____
_____
_____
_____
_____
_____
_____
_____
_____
_____
_____
_____
_____

AUTHENTICITY OR FACADE

PART THREE

Esther 3:4-5
*Now it was when they had spoken daily to him and he would
not listen to them, that they told Haman to see whether Mordecai's reason would stand; for he had told them that he was
a Jew. When Haman saw that Mordecai neither bowed down
nor paid homage to him, Haman was filled with rage.*

Mordecai, Esther's guardian, would not bow to any man. As a Jew, he bowed
only to the one true God. Not only was Haman's authority challenged, but
his ego was shattered. Kindled by Mordecai's disobedience to the king's
command to pay homage to Haman, and what he considered antagonism,
Haman's anger turned to rage.

Throughout the ages men have sought to destroy God's chosen people. Haman is another in the long line of arrogant men who, whether knowing it or
not, fought against God by attempting to annihilate the Jews.

Bad choice Haman. God wins.

God wins in our lives as well when we are faced with what seems to be insurmountable obstacles. Whether personal or professional, when we take our
circumstances before God's throne and leave them with Him, He is faithful
to deliver His beloved people in ways only He is able. And often in unimaginable ways.

JOURNAL

If challenged, would you stand firm in your faith? ~ How?

_____
_____
_____
_____
_____

What makes you determined to cling to your faith?

_____
_____
_____
_____
_____
_____
_____
_____
_____

What is your heart whispering?

_____
_____
_____
_____
_____
_____
_____
_____
_____
_____
_____
_____
_____
_____
_____
_____
_____

AUTHENTICITY OR FACADE
PART FOUR

Esther 4:15-16
Then Esther told them to reply to Mordecai, "Go, assemble all the Jews who are found in Susa, and fast for me; do not eat or drink for three days, night or day. I and my maidens also will fast in the same way. And thus I will go in to the king, which is not according to the law; and if I perish, I perish."

When Hadassah, now known as Queen Esther, learns of Haman's evil plot to kill Mordecai and destroy every Jew in the kingdom, Mordecai directs her to plead with the king for the lives of her people. Though against kingdom protocol, Esther agrees, asking Mordecai and all the Jews to fast with her for three days before she enters the king's presence. Although the passage does not mention God, His intervention is inferred when the Jewish custom of fasting is called. The Jews pray and fast asking God for wisdom and direction.

Esther secretly plans to expose Haman by pretending to honor him with two banquets inviting only King Ahasuerus and Haman. This invitation proves to swell Haman's pride. And in a fit of rage, at Mordecai's refusal to honor him, Haman resolves to hang Mordecai on the morning of the second banquet.

As they say in mysteries, 'the plot thickens.'

But God . . . What other explanation is there for how the king discovers the one record in the kingdom's chronicles of Mordecai having saved the king's life? Surprisingly, Haman, thinking the king desires to honor him, puts into motion a plan that ultimately honors Mordecai.

Gotta love how God intervenes for those who choose to honor Him with their lives. Often God intervenes in small personal ways that may not change the circumstances, but rather, changes the person. When we surrender our lives to God, His transformation of conforming us to the image of our King, Jesus Christ, begins.

Yes indeed, 'the plot thickens'.

DAY FOUR

JOURNAL

How would you end this story?

_____
_____
_____
_____
_____

Would you change the plot ~ How?

_____
_____
_____
_____
_____
_____
_____
_____
_____

What is your heart whispering?

_____
_____
_____
_____
_____
_____
_____
_____
_____
_____
_____
_____
_____
_____
_____
_____
_____
_____

AUTHENTICITY OR FACADE
PART FIVE

Esther 9:29-31
Then Queen Esther, daughter of Abihail, with Mordecai the Jew, wrote with full authority to confirm this second letter about Purim. He sent letters to all the Jews, to the 127 provinces of the kingdom of Ahasuerus, namely, words of peace and truth, to establish these days of Purim at their appointed times, just as Mordecai the Jew and Queen Esther had established for them, and just as they had established for themselves and for their descendants with instructions for their times of fasting and their lamentations.

A person who is authentic, is genuine, honest, real; one who is courageous enough to tell the truth when faced with contrary challenges or defiant opposition.

Conversely, one who presents a façade, is a proponent of falsehood and artificial counterfeit actions.

Truth versus lies. Sincerity versus hypocrisy. Blameless versus guilty. Authentic versus façade. All of this begs the question once again, what is behind the façade?

As the story in the book of Esther plays out, we could surmise any number of behind-the-scenes scenarios for the actions of the people involved. One thing is clear, when insecurity, deceit, and greed are behind the façade, the ending is rarely promising. Rather truth, honesty and authenticity causes the possessor to welcome the outcome.

Perhaps the better question for us might be, do we want to present a life that exhibits a façade or live out a life of true authenticity and integrity?

JOURNAL

Write a short story (fiction or non-fiction) with the plot of good triumphing over evil.

_____
_____
_____
_____
_____
_____
_____
_____
_____
_____
_____

Transform one of your evil characters into a hero.

_____
_____
_____
_____
_____
_____
_____
_____

What is your heart whispering?

_____
_____
_____
_____
_____
_____
_____
_____
_____
_____
_____

BIRDS HAVE A HOME

Psalm 84:3
The bird also has found a house, and the swallow a nest for herself, where she may lay her young, even Your altars, O LORD of hosts, my King and my God.

Matthew 6:26
Look at the birds of the air, that they do not sow, nor reap nor gather into barns, and yet your heavenly Father feeds them. Are you not worth much more than they?

Ah yes, the birds. They carry no baggage as they travel through life. We however, fret and worry, plan and contrive to make things happen. Why, when we have a heavenly Father who cares for every detail of our lives? He cares not simply for birds, but for all of His creation.

Watch the birds. God speaks bird-language and directs them to their home, to a safe haven. Albeit temporary, God provides a place to hatch their young and give them shelter.

God created each of the birds unique to their own species. Some chatter with a voluminous flock in trees. Larger species scratch the earth and run for safety. Others soar through the sky catching the wind. Still others fly in formation to gain the wind current for those who follow. Each with God's purpose.

Unique. Going. Doing. Being. According to His purpose. So like us. Without anxiety we choose to follow Him, trusting He has a place for us to nest. Trusting that our heavenly Father will direct our days with His sovereign, wise rule.

JOURNAL

Slow down and look around, life is happening everywhere.
What do you see?

_____

_____

_____

_____

_____

_____

_____

_____

_____

_____

What astounds you about God's vibrant creation?

_____

_____

_____

_____

_____

_____

_____

_____

_____

_____

What is your heart whispering?

_____

_____

_____

_____

_____

_____

_____

_____

_____

_____

_____

_____

_____

BOLD HUMBLE JOB

Job 40:1-6a, 8
*Then the LORD said to Job, "Will the faultfinder contend
with the Almighty? Let him who reproves God answer it."
Then Job answered the LORD and said, "Behold, I am insignificant; what can I reply to You? I lay my hand on my mouth.
Once I have spoken, and I will not answer; even twice, and I
will add nothing more." Then the LORD answered Job out of
the storm and said . . . "Will you really annul My judgment?
Will you condemn Me that you may be justified?"*

Wow. Really Job?
Yet it is so like us, don't you think? Attempting to reject or cast off the blame
to justify our actions and make ourselves look good.

After Job's prolonged diatribe of defense to his 'friends', the LORD con-
fronts him with myriad questions. Does Job understand who God is? Does he
realize all the miraculous things God has done? Can his finite brain comprehend the feats of an infinite God?

It always astonishes me how bold Job is when he speaks to God. But more
than that I am amazed at Job's humble, repentant heart, revealing he is indeed
the man God described to Satan in Job 1:8. Even when the enemy accuses
us and lies to us, we know, and have seen time and again, God is faithful.
ALWAYS.

Paul knew it and told the Romans as much in his missive to them ~
What then? If some did not believe, their unbelief will not nullify the faithfulness of God, will it? May it never be! Rather, let God be found true,
though every man be found a liar.*

True that.

*Romans 3:3-4a

JOURNAL

God knows what is happening in your life ~ He wants you to be bold and honest. Share your hurts, frustrations, and heart's desire with Him ~ He will surprise you with His responses.

_____
_____
_____
_____
_____
_____
_____
_____
_____
_____
_____
_____
_____
_____
_____
_____
_____
_____
_____
_____
_____
_____
_____

What is your heart whispering?

_____
_____
_____
_____
_____
_____
_____

DO NOT DOUBT

James 1:2-6
Consider it all joy, my brethren, when you encounter various trials, knowing that the testing of your faith produces endurance. And let endurance have its perfect result, so that you may be perfect and complete, lacking in nothing. But if any of you lacks wisdom, let him ask of God, who gives to all generously and without reproach, and it will be given to him. But he must ask in faith without any doubting, for the one who doubts is like the surf of the sea, driven and tossed by the wind.

Ever felt this way? A wave moving steadily forward to gently play out on the shore and suddenly a heavy blustering wind rolls in. As the wave crests it is violently tossed about and crashes ferociously into the rocks. This is what *doubting God can feel like. We begin by knowing, trusting that we are moving in the direction He has planned, then something happens that causes us to pull back and hesitate, to wonder.

Did we really hear God? Was this simply a personal desire we wanted to see come to fruition? Are we doubting in the natural what God is doing in the supernatural?

Yes, the enemy of our souls would like nothing better than to cause us to doubt God, and to question how He causes all things to work together for good to those who love Him and are called according to His purpose.**

God never promised we would see everything He sees. However, He does encourage us to have faith. Even when there are tumultuous circumstances and unknown outcomes, He wants us to know that His hand is on our lives and for us to move forward without doubting.

*Webster's Online Dictionary
doubt - a state of affairs giving rise to uncertainty, hesitation . . .
**Romans 8:28

DAY EIGHT

JOURNAL

How about you ~ what is happening in your life that is causing you to doubt God?

_____

_____

_____

_____

_____

_____

_____

_____

How do you go from doubt to absolute assurance and trust?

_____

_____

_____

_____

_____

_____

_____

_____

_____

_____

_____

_____

_____

_____

What is your heart whispering?

_____

_____

_____

_____

_____

_____

_____

_____

_____

_____

DO YOU CALL ME LORD?

Luke 6:46
"Why do you call Me, 'Lord, Lord,' and do not do what I say?"

Jesus is proclaiming a profound message to His disciples and, what the Bible calls 'a great throng of people'. He is teaching them what the life of His disciple ought to look like. Near the end of His discourse Jesus, in effect, reprimands them for their lip service.

I have to wonder as Jesus looked out at the large crowd if He knew which people in the crowd were poor, sick, possessed, devious, arrogant, insincere? If He spoke to what He saw? If maybe He watched their eyes, their body language and knew the depths of their hearts?

What occupies the depth of our hearts? Jesus still speaks today to our spirit, through His word, circumstances, other people, the Holy Spirit. We who belong to Jesus can know what our Lord is saying. But do we go forth in His strength? Are we following our Father's merciful example? Do we understand Jesus' gracious words and actions? Are we listening to the Holy Spirit's wisdom?

Previously, while in the synagogue, Jesus read aloud a portion of Isaiah's writings and basically told the people that He was the much anticipated Messiah Isaiah had spoken of. Shouldn't we who love Jesus and call Him Lord, proclaim that He is Messiah and share what He has done for all mankind? We ought to be excited to do what He says.

JOURNAL

What person might you be in this large crowd?

_____

_____

_____

_____

_____

_____

Is there something hidden in your life that does not honor Jesus as Lord?

_____

_____

_____

_____

_____

What will you do with it now that you have recognized and acknowledged it?

_____

_____

_____

_____

_____

_____

_____

What is your heart whispering?

_____

_____

_____

_____

_____

_____

_____

_____

_____

FIRST LOVE

Revelation 2:4-5a   AMP
But I have this [charge] against you, that you have left your
first love [you have lost the depth of love that you first had for
Me]. So remember the heights from which you have fallen,
and repent [change your inner self—your old way of thinking,
your sinful behavior—seek God's will] and do the works you
did at first [when you first knew Me].

Oh, the reality of honest conviction. We often confuse conviction with guilt. Guilt tells us we are bad people for what we've done, for how we live. The Holy Spirit's conviction is not meant to heap guilt upon us. It is meant to lovingly reveal the truth of what is going on in our lives, in our hearts, so that we can admit our mistakes, our sins. We have the opportunity to repent, renounce and turn away from them, through the power of the Holy Spirit.

We get to do this when our love for God far exceeds our desire to continue relishing the sin.

When we remember the miracle of love for Jesus that captivated us when we first knew Him, our intimate depth of love that grew making Him first in our lives above all else, we long for even more.

Sensing the Holy Spirit's conviction is a divine gift, calling us away from every distraction that has drawn us from our first love. Our attention and focus ecstatically shifts to where it belongs ~ Jesus.

DAY TEN

JOURNAL

Define conviction.

_____
_____
_____
_____
_____
_____

Define guilt.

_____
_____
_____
_____
_____

How have those things distracted you from Jesus, your first love?

_____
_____
_____
_____
_____
_____
_____

What is your heart whispering?

_____
_____
_____
_____
_____
_____
_____
_____
_____

FOUR PROFOUND WORDS

Genesis 1:1
In the beginning God . . .

Four profound words to contemplate and deliberate.
God is real. Even if we don't embrace that truth, it is still true.

Intellectually ~ One might admit after much study, calculation, and research something or Someone exists that created all that surrounds us. Some choose to embrace the lie that there is no God, that we are gods unto ourselves and we make our own way in life without the help or need of a supreme, sovereign being.

Emotionally ~ There are those whose reality seems to be that all our emotions and senses have been evolved from pond scum. These people choose to believe this fantasy.

Spiritually ~ Consider this, we are spiritual beings living in a physical body. Our souls will live forever in one of two places - heaven or hell. Our loving omniscient, omnipotent, omnipresent God has graciously given us a choice where we spend eternity. Some choose heaven . . . by choosing Jesus*.

Physically ~ Some are determined to prove our body's design can be explained through scientific suppositions. Really? Have you ever looked at the minute intricacy of the human body and how every part relies on the other parts to work in harmony to even work at all?

Challenge ~ Look at the workings of one part of the body-the eyes. You will be hard-pressed not to believe God is real. You might even find you have cause to question scientific hypotheses.

Lord make Yourself real to people in unique ways as only You are able. May they see You as the beginning and the eternal end.

* John 14:6

JOURNAL

What do these four words mean to you? ~ In the beginning God . . .

_____

_____

_____

_____

How do they affect your life today?

_____

_____

_____

_____

_____

What do you think a scientist who is a Christian would believe?

_____

_____

_____

_____

_____

_____

_____

What is your heart whispering?

_____

_____

_____

_____

_____

_____

_____

_____

_____

_____

_____

FROM SIGNIFICANCE TO ANONYMITY
PART ONE

Luke 18:40-41a   AMP
Then Jesus stopped and ordered that the blind man be led to
Him; and when he came near, Jesus asked him, "What do you
want Me to do for you?"

This brief encounter with Jesus is packed with lessons for us today. In just these two verses we are taught, once again, what real love looks like.

Jesus, traveling with His disciples, stopped everything to care for one man. In the midst of the raucous crowd Jesus heard the agonizing cry of a hopeless beggar, the least of the least. Even though the man's need was obvious, Jesus asks a poignant question, "What do you want Me to do for you?"

Doesn't He ask the same of us today? He wants us to stop and look deep into our souls for the real eternal need. However, we often simply reply with the immediate physical need.

Since this man asks to regain his sight, it is quite possible he once lived a vibrant productive life. But with the loss of sight, he became a beggar crying out for just enough to survive. One might surmise that a part of his longing to regain his vision was to recapture his place in society. He quite possibly had gone from significance to anonymity. Could it be he wanted his life back?

DAY TWELVE

JOURNAL

People are important to God. Why was this man significant even in his hopeless situation?

_____
_____
_____
_____
_____
_____

What can you do to show people they have significance?

_____
_____
_____
_____
_____
_____
_____
_____
_____
_____
_____
_____
_____
_____

What is your heart whispering?

_____
_____
_____
_____
_____
_____
_____
_____
_____
_____
_____

FROM SIGNIFICANCE TO ANONYMITY
PART TWO

Luke 18:40b-41 AMP
Jesus asked him, "What do you want Me to do for you?" He
said, "Lord, let me regain my sight!"

You have to wonder if the man really believed Jesus could do the impossible and give him back his sight. Would Jesus even hear his cry for relief from his poverty, in the midst of the vast crowd?

Jesus stopped everything else to speak to the broken, bereft beggar and honor him with a listening ear while others in the crowd degraded the man by sternly telling him to keep quiet. He called out all the more, desperate for Jesus to hear him, to see him, to show him mercy. Jesus saw the man's true need, to know, receive and follow his Savior.

When Jesus grants the man's petition, He lets everyone know it was the man's faith that gave him the desire of his heart.

There are those who are silently screaming for significance if we would simply take the time to see. To look into the eyes of someone in the crowd, to truly see them, and ask God to reveal their need. Shouldn't we follow Jesus' example and care enough to stop everything, and if God encourages nothing else, offer a silent prayer? Then thank God for His perfect answer.

JOURNAL

Do we stop from our hectic day to day busy-ness to see the need of others who are crying out?

_____
_____
_____
_____
_____

What would that look like for you?

_____
_____
_____
_____
_____

What will you do with God's encouragement to honor those considered insignificant?

_____
_____
_____
_____
_____
_____
_____
_____

What is your heart whispering?

_____
_____
_____
_____
_____
_____
_____
_____
_____

GOD MAKES A WAY

Nehemiah 9:5b, 6

"Arise, bless the LORD your God forever and ever! O may Your glorious name be blessed and exalted above all blessing and praise! You alone are the LORD. You have made the heavens, the heaven of heavens with all their host, the earth and all that is on it, the seas and all that is in them. You give life to all of them and the heavenly host bows down before You."

God makes a way when there seems to be no way. Time and again God shows Himself as the God of impossibilities. His faithfulness never fails.

The book of Nehemiah is filled with examples of God's supernatural miraculous ways. Recognizing God's wonders, Nehemiah shouts praises exalting the LORD God Almighty.

Thinking of things this morning that look impossible in my own life, God graciously reminds me through His word that nothing is impossible for Him. He is able and will accomplish what concerns me.

Throughout the Bible, God reveals His power by continually doing the miraculous. Something supernatural only God can do, by the way.

Are you excited to see God make a way where there seems to be no way in your own circumstances?

JOURNAL

What impossible things would you like to see God turn into possibilities?

_____
_____
_____
_____
_____
_____

Be bold ~ ask Him ~ He always answers.

_____
_____
_____
_____
_____
_____
_____
_____
_____
_____
_____
_____
_____

What is your heart whispering?

_____
_____
_____
_____
_____
_____
_____
_____
_____
_____
_____

HEAVY HEART PRAYING

Exodus 15:11
*Who is like You among the gods, O LORD? Who is like You,
majestic in holiness, awesome in praises, working wonders?*

Jeremiah 31:3
*The LORD appeared to him from afar, saying, "I have loved
you with an everlasting love; therefore, I have drawn you
with lovingkindness {unfailing love*}."*

God has put someone on my heart this morning and the heaviness isn't going
away. Someone who refuses to acknowledge who God is and His majestic
glory. If God is doing likewise with you for someone, please stop everything
else you are doing and pray for that person.

This is my prayer . . .

Lord, this person is heavy on my heart this morning. Jesus, by the
power of Your mighty name, free them from their prison. The prison
of despondent desperation, depression, despair. This person has tried
everything to fill the emptiness, the dark hole of despair that grows
wider and deeper with each day. Jesus, make Yourself real to them.
Cause them to seek Your majesty.

Like the apostle, Paul, on the road to Damascus, show this person
Your glory. Call their heart to You. Release this one from the lying
clutches of the enemy who would keep them in the darkness, tempt
ing them to try every kind of thing to appease and diminish the
excruciating pain they feel. Cause them to open Your living word and
experience You.

Show them that Your promises are REAL Lord.

Amen.

*New Living Translation

DAY FIFTEEN

JOURNAL

Ask God to show you how to pray for _____.

_____
_____
_____
_____
_____
_____
_____

Ask Him what you are to pray for this person.

_____
_____
_____
_____
_____

What is your heart whispering?

_____
_____
_____
_____
_____
_____
_____
_____
_____
_____
_____
_____
_____
_____
_____
_____
_____
_____

HOPE RENEWED

2 Corinthians 10:3-5   NCV
We do live in the world, but we do not fight in the same way the world fights. We fight with weapons that are different from those the world uses. Our weapons have power from God that can destroy the enemy's strong places. We destroy people's arguments and every proud thing that raises itself against the knowledge of God. We capture every thought and make it give up and obey Christ.

As I write this, my thoughts and emotions abound as every aspect of life is shifting. All the things I've taken for granted as being the everyday norm are in question. My thoughts tend to run rampant. How will this new norm manifest? Will it run its course and the pendulum come back to the center of normal? Or is this new societal normal a more degraded and less holy one I must adapt to?

Here's what I know. When my thoughts begin to move in the wrong direction of 'what if' I am drawn even more to the truth of God's word. Paul's admonition to remember how our battle is fought and Who fights it, reminds me to reel in those thoughts of what might happen and speak aloud words of truth about my loving God's sovereign rule.

In this uncertain time, shifting those fear-based thoughts to God-powered truths, are needed several times a day. The encouragement of other believers plays a significant role in keeping my thoughts where they ought to be. And as my thoughts shift to God's truth, I can pass the encouragement along to others.

Hope is renewed. Focus shifted. Reality realized. Fear annihilated. God glorified.

JOURNAL

What can you do to shift your focus when fearful thoughts take over?

_____
_____
_____
_____
_____
_____

Who can you call upon to share your concerns and to pray with you?

_____
_____
_____
_____
_____
_____
_____
_____
_____
_____
_____
_____
_____
_____

What is your heart whispering?

_____
_____
_____
_____
_____
_____
_____
_____
_____
_____
_____

IS THIS THE WAY

Psalm 143:8-10
Let me hear Your lovingkindness {unfailing love} in the
morning; for I trust in You; teach me the way in which I
should walk; for to You I lift up my soul. Deliver me, O
LORD, from my enemies; I take refuge in You. Teach me to do
Your will, for You are my God; let Your good Spirit lead me
on level ground.*

What a great prayer to start the day. David begins this psalm by asking God
to hear his prayer. Then he pours out his heart anguishing over the painful
struggles in his life.

David reminds himself of the things God has done in the past and tells Him
how much he longs for His presence in a land that is parched {barren of wa-
ter, literally thirsting for God}. He asks desperately for God's help and to be
able to hear Him. Then David listens.

Remembering who his God is, David asks how he should live his life. He
asks because he knows he can rely on God to be his refuge, and desires for
the Spirit, who has all wisdom, to lead him.

Yes, Lord, may we come to You remembering who You are, what You've
done, how gracious Your love is and not take a step without asking if this is
the way we are to walk.

*New Living Translation

JOURNAL

Write out your own prayer with~
Praise

_____
_____
_____
_____

Worship

_____
_____
_____
_____

Selfless repentance

_____
_____
_____
_____

Honorable requests

_____
_____
_____
_____

What is your heart whispering?

_____
_____
_____
_____
_____
_____
_____
_____

JOY OF GOD'S REJOICING

Zephaniah 3:17
The LORD your God is in your midst, a victorious warrior.
He will exult over you with joy, He will renew you in His love,
He will rejoice over you with shouts of joy.

Zephaniah's prophecy is for Israel ~ Jerusalem specifically. Yet it is also for all of God's people. And that includes believers in Jesus Christ. We have been adopted into Israel's family. Grafted in.

This passage always makes me smile. To remember God, my victorious warrior, is here with me now. And He exults* over me with joy, reminding me daily in unique ways of His great love. He rejoices with shouts of joy.

Can't you just envision God smiling down at us? God's profound love extends to all humanity if they would but receive it. It goes far beyond our limited time here, on into eternity. Eternity.

Life always boils down to God's love, doesn't it? Will we believe it and receive it or not? Surely if people knew, they would want God in their midst rejoicing and exulting over them.

*Noah Webster's 1828 Dictionary - Exult - to leap for joy; hence, to rejoice in triumph; to rejoice exceedingly at success or victory; to be glad above measure; to triumph

JOURNAL

Have you chosen to receive God's profound love?

_____

_____

_____

_____

How is God's love different from any other love?

_____

_____

_____

_____

How can you share this joyous God with others?

_____

_____

_____

_____

What is your heart whispering?

_____

_____

_____

_____

_____

_____

_____

_____

_____

_____

_____

_____

_____

_____

_____

_____

_____

_____

_____

_____

LIVE LIKE CHRIST IS YOUR LIFE

Galatians 5:25 AMP
*If we [claim to] live by the [Holy] Spirit, we must also walk
by the Spirit [with personal integrity, godly character, and
moral courage—our conduct empowered by the Holy Spirit].*

If . . . no since, Christ is my life, I need to live like it and bring every choice, every decision to my all-wise best friend, the Holy Spirit. He enables me and provides the supernatural power needed to live the holy life God desires. He shapes my character as I obey His directives. It's an easy thing to do when He graciously reminds me to whom I belong and what Christ Jesus has done for me. Not to mention His power works in me as we walk through life together.

For, in reality, the selfish woman who lived before I knew Christ, seeking only to ingratiate herself to others, to look good on the outside when inside there was a craving for real life, is no longer living. I scarcely know, but am beginning to appreciate, this new creature who now loves and serves Christ.

The Father, the Son, and the Holy Spirit are preeminent in this new life. They take precedence over everything else.

Ergo my mantra, since Christ is my life . . . live like it!

DAY NINETEEN

JOURNAL

What must you do to actually live like Christ is your life?

_____

_____

_____

_____

_____

_____

_____

What is churning inside you that needs to be recognized, faced and removed permanently from your life?

_____

_____

_____

_____

_____

_____

What is your heart whispering?

_____

_____

_____

_____

_____

_____

_____

_____

_____

_____

_____

_____

_____

MARCHING ORDERS

Joshua 1:2, 6, 11
*The LORD spoke to Joshua . . . "Moses My servant is dead;
now therefore arise, cross this Jordan, you and all this
people, to the land which I am giving to them, to the sons of
Israel . . ."Be strong and courageous, for you shall give this
people possession of the land which I swore to their fathers to
give them . . ."Pass through the midst of the camp and command the people, saying, 'Prepare provisions for yourselves,
for within three days you are to cross this Jordan, to go in to
possess the land which the LORD your God is giving you, to
possess it.'"*

God gave Joshua his marching orders. After wandering aimlessly in the wil-
derness for 40 years it was time to move forward. Time to claim the promise
God said would take place. The command to be ready to go in three days
must have been a shock to the people.

Everything they were commanded to do was nestled under the protective
umbrella of ~ TRUST GOD.

Go ~ Claim God's Promises ~ Prepare to Move Forward

After all those years of God's plentiful provision and protection would the
people believe it was time to possess the land God promised Moses? There
was no time to waste, in three days they would stand on the shore of the Jordan River. Knowing confrontation and battles probably awaited them in this
promised land, the people chose to trust God and go.

Often we get comfortable and complacent in the place where we've land-
ed. Perhaps God has revealed there is more {it could be an actual physical
place, a spiritual move, an emotional change} yet we cannot see it. Then God
makes it clear it is time to move forward.

JOURNAL

Will you trust God, take the first step, and go?

_____
_____
_____
_____
_____
_____
_____

What does that first step look like for you?

_____
_____
_____
_____
_____
_____
_____

What is your heart whispering?

_____
_____
_____
_____
_____
_____
_____
_____
_____
_____
_____
_____
_____
_____
_____

NEHEMIAH'S STORY

Nehemiah 1:4-6a
*When I heard these words, I sat down and wept and mourned
for days; and I was fasting and praying before the God of
heaven. I said, "I beseech You, O LORD God of heaven, the
great and awesome God, who preserves the covenant and
lovingkindness {unfailing love*} for those who love Him and
keep His commandments, let Your ear now be attentive and
Your eyes open to hear the prayer of Your servant which I am
praying before You now, day and night.*

Can we even imagine how deeply Nehemiah loved the Jews that remained
in Jerusalem? His disappointment for the distress and reproach they were
receiving must have been overwhelming.

Nehemiah is such a great example of how to handle desperation and disappointment. He stopped everything else and cried out to God. The One true
God, who had more than once in the past, poured out compassion, wisdom
and mercy on His people.

After four months of continual prayer asking for God's intervention for his
people, Nehemiah, as the king's **cupbearer, brought his sorrowful coun-
tenance before King Artaxerxes. The king obviously respected Nehemiah
when he acknowledged his sadness and trusted him by allowing him to go to
Jerusalem and rebuild the wall.

Nehemiah's story is one of integrity, favor and complete trust in the power
of his God. Prayer takes precedence over every part of Nehemiah's life as is
evident through his example to the remnant in Jerusalem.

Prayer takes us into God's presence, allowing a deeper intimacy with Him.
Prayer releases supernatural power on earth as it is in heaven.

*New Living Translation
**tester of wine to be sure the king was not being poisoned

DAY TWENTY-ONE

JOURNAL

Are you feeling desperate and disappointed? How would you ask God to intervene?

_____
_____
_____
_____
_____
_____
_____

What would it look like if you allowed God to reveal His power in ways only He is able?

_____
_____
_____
_____
_____
_____
_____

What is your heart whispering?

_____
_____
_____
_____
_____
_____
_____
_____
_____
_____
_____
_____
_____
_____

ONE TRUE CALL

Daniel 4:29-30
*Twelve months later he (King Nebuchadnezzar) was walking
on the roof of the royal palace of Babylon. The king reflected
and said, 'Is this not Babylon the great, which I myself have
built as a royal residence by the might of my power and for
the glory of my majesty?'*

How easily we begin to believe 'our own press' until something happens to
cause us to question reality. King Nebuchadnezzar is certainly a good case in
point. Throughout Nebuchadnezzar's story, as told in the book of Daniel, he
believes himself to be above all the gods he professes to serve, showing his
arrogance and pride. Even after the fiery furnace incident, and Daniel's inter-
pretation of Nebuchadnezzar's dream, not to mention the prophecies Daniel
gave of the future, the king is blind to reality.

Believing himself all-powerful over all his natural realm, Nebuchadnezzar
saw only what others praised and what he himself believed as truth. Oh, he
acknowledged the God of the Hebrews as having power, just not as omnipotent.

Enter Daniel.

Through Daniel God warned Nebuchadnezzar, giving him the opportunity to
turn from his sins and confess that the God of heaven rules the earth. Instead,
Nebuchadnezzar's pride took hold, and he ignored the word of the Most High
God. Not long after, Nebuchadnezzar's idea of his calling was turned upside
down.

Daniel 4:34-35
*"But at the end of that period, I, Nebuchadnezzar, raised
my eyes toward heaven and my reason returned to me, and
I blessed the Most High and praised and honored Him who
lives forever; for His dominion is an everlasting dominion,
and His kingdom endures from generation to generation. All
the inhabitants of the earth are accounted as nothing, but He
does according to His will in the host of heaven and among
the inhabitants of earth; and no one can strike against His
hand or say to Him, "What have You done?"*

DAY TWENTY-TWO

JOURNAL

What decision can you make today to believe God?

_____
_____
_____
_____
_____
_____
_____

How can you honor God with that decision?

_____
_____
_____
_____
_____
_____
_____

What is your heart whispering?

_____
_____
_____
_____
_____
_____
_____
_____
_____
_____
_____
_____
_____
_____
_____

PLIABLE VESSEL IN GOD'S HANDS

Isaiah 64:8
*But now, O LORD, You are our Father, we are the clay, and
You our potter; and all of us are the work of Your hand.*

Romans 9:21
*Or does not the potter have a right over the clay, to make
from the same lump one vessel for honorable use and another
for common use?*

*Pliable is the word that comes to mind when envisioning a lump of clay.
Consider all the uses for clay in Isaiah's day and Paul's, as well as today. Vessels to drink from, cook with, service vessels. And if made with the proper
components clay can be used as a type of mortar to connect and hold together
other pieces of clay.

Could it be God has various uses for us as His vessels, depending on the
season of our lives, the place He moves us, the people around us? Are we
willing to be malleable in His strong, tender hands? Even when He reshapes
us for use in the new and possibly uncertain circumstances we now find ourselves? Even if it is for common use?

Truly the whirling of the potter's wheel can cause dizzying uncertainty. We
don't know what the end result will be. Yet for us, as God's Beloved, we can
be assured it will end up honoring Him . . . if we are **supple in His hands.

Father, may we release our preconceived ideas of what Your vessel ought to
be and ask You to mold us, shape us, transform us.

Webster's Online Dictionary
*pliable - supple enough to bend freely or repeatedly without breaking
**supple - readily adaptable or responsive to new situations

DAY TWENTY-THREE

JOURNAL

Have you found yourself stiff and unbending in the season you are in?

_____
_____
_____
_____
_____
_____
_____

What is God calling you to do to become pliable and supple to follow His will?

_____
_____
_____
_____
_____
_____
_____

What is your heart whispering?

_____
_____
_____
_____
_____
_____
_____
_____
_____
_____
_____
_____
_____
_____
_____

PSALM 117 PARAPHRASE

Psalm 117   NLT
*Praise the LORD, all you nations. Praise Him, all you people
of the earth. For His unfailing love for us is powerful; the
LORD'S faithfulness endures forever. Praise the LORD!*

Sometimes there is a deep desire to make God's word personal.

Anne's paraphrase of Psalm 117.

Glorify the Sovereign I AM, all the empires, kingdoms, nations. May every
person living on this planet magnify Him by extolling His majestic presence.
His mantle of never-ending, unconditional love enfolds us and ignites insatia-
ble longings for more of Him. My soul offers untold gratitude to the God of
the universe for His life-giving, enduring, eternal truth.

JOURNAL

Try it yourself. Find a passage in Scripture that speaks to your soul and paraphrase it ~ make is personal.

_____
_____
_____
_____
_____
_____
_____
_____
_____
_____
_____
_____
_____
_____
_____
_____
_____

What is your heart whispering?

_____
_____
_____
_____
_____
_____
_____
_____
_____
_____
_____
_____
_____
_____
_____
_____
_____
_____
_____
_____

PSALM 150

Psalm 150
Praise the LORD!
Praise God in His sanctuary;
Praise Him in His mighty expanse. Praise Him for His mighty
deeds; praise Him according to His excellent greatness.
Praise Him with trumpet sound; praise Him with harp and
lyre.
Praise Him with timbrel and dancing; praise Him with
stringed instruments and pipe.
Praise Him with loud cymbals; praise Him with resounding
cymbals.
Let everything that has breath praise the LORD.
Praise the LORD!

Have you ever watched God's creation praise Him in their own unique way? I remember walking among several cottonwood trees when a subtle breeze came up and I could hear the leaves clapping together like they were giving Him praise.

Look at the ocean with its vast expanse and how the waves rise up. The sea creatures with their various sounds and designs are incredibly vivacious in their attempt to give God praise.

The sun, moon and stars praise God every morning throughout the day on into the night hours.

Look around you. Everything God created praises Him in their own remarkable way.

Can we do any less with this precious life God has given us? Come on y'all, let every breath praise Him.

JOURNAL

Find something in nature that praises God.

_____
_____
_____
_____

Describe something you've seen a person do to praise God.

_____
_____
_____
_____

Discover a new way for you, yourself to praise God.

_____
_____
_____
_____

Start a praise journal with entries morning and night.

What is your heart whispering?

_____
_____
_____
_____
_____
_____
_____
_____
_____
_____
_____
_____
_____
_____
_____
_____
_____
_____
_____

PURIFYING GRACE

PART ONE

Titus 2:11-14

For the grace of God has appeared, bringing salvation to all
men, instructing us to deny ungodliness and worldly desires
and to live sensibly, righteously and godly in the present age,
looking for the blessed hope and the appearing of the glory
of our great God and Savior, Christ Jesus, who gave Himself
for us to redeem us from every lawless deed, and to purify for
Himself a people for His own possession, zealous for good
deeds.

Once we comprehend why Jesus gave Himself to be crucified on the cross to save us, how could we even consider refusing the Father's gracious gift of salvation? As the apostle Paul says, "May it never be."

When we claim this life-changing gift, we begin a lifelong transformation process. Just like purifying gold to refine it to its purest form, God takes His own beloved heirs through the cleansing process so that we will live out our faith, honoring Him and drawing others to Jesus.

What then is the result of the grace of God that brings about this purification? A bond-servant, as Paul describes it, of Jesus Christ, zealous for good deeds.

We are a special treasure to Jesus Christ, His own possession. What a precious name to be called. What a sweet place to live, tucked safely in the reality that we belong to Him.

But as His own, why must He purify us? We are human beings, born into a sinful world that desperately needs a Savior. In this passage, Paul explains that Jesus voluntarily offered His life as a sacrifice to redeem us from every unholy deed; as well as from the sin that contaminates our souls and draws our faith farther away from experiencing the truth of God's promises.

Not a pretty picture. Nor is that the life Jesus desires for us.

JOURNAL

Ask God to reveal anything in your life that needs purification.

_____
_____
_____
_____

How do you think the refining process will change you?

_____
_____
_____
_____
_____
_____
_____

Journal daily what the changes and transformation looks and feels like.

What is your heart whispering?

_____
_____
_____
_____
_____
_____
_____
_____
_____
_____
_____
_____
_____
_____
_____
_____
_____
_____

PURIFYING GRACE

PART TWO

Titus 2:11-14 AMP
For the [remarkable, undeserved] grace of God that brings salvation has appeared to all men. It teaches us to reject ungodliness and worldly (immoral) desires, and to live sensible, upright, and godly lives [with a purpose that reflect spiritual maturity] in this present age, awaiting and confidently expecting the [fulfillment of our] blessed hope and the glorious appearing of our great God and Savior, Christ Jesus, who [willingly] gave Himself [to be crucified] on our behalf to redeem us and purchase our freedom from all wickedness, and to purify for Himself a chosen and very special people to be His own possession, who are enthusiastic for doing what is good.

We know this grace Paul describes has us looking for the blessed hope of seeing the glory of Christ Jesus when He returns. And return He will, in all His glory*.

In the meantime we are to receive training through God's grace, gladly putting His instruction into practice. Through God's power alone we are able to, as Paul puts it, reject ungodliness and worldly desires. We can live godly lives right where we are, right now.

For God so loved the world . . . and poured out His grace for every person.
For just as God said when I asked, "What did You make me to be?"
His loving response was, "I made you to be Mine."

*Revelation 19:11-16

DAY TWENTY-SEVEN

JOURNAL

How can you receive this training Paul alludes to?

_____

_____

_____

_____

Training would indicate more than one person involved ~ can you think of someone who would be willing to give you instruction in living a God honoring life?

_____

_____

_____

_____

_____

_____

_____

What is your heart whispering?

_____

_____

_____

_____

_____

_____

_____

_____

_____

_____

_____

_____

_____

_____

_____

_____

_____

TAKE RESPONSIBILITY FOR OUR ACTIONS

Proverbs 19:3   GNT
*Some people ruin themselves by their own stupid actions and
then blame the LORD.*

Oh, we are such inconsistent, unaccountable people. Does this irresponsibility come from our DNA stemming from the original audacious, defiant pair in the Garden of Eden? Why is it so difficult for us to take responsibility for our actions rather than blaming others? Often blaming God.

Humility lacking, we choose justified vindication, desiring our persona to reflect perfection (an impossibility for human beings by the way).

For some, this suggests narcissism. Not only ruining themselves as this proverb says, but degrading others by causing them to feel imperfect, flawed. If they don't have another person to blame then of course, it must be God's fault.

Thank You Father for Your Son, the only perfect human ~ EVER. Jesus not only gave us a living example of true humility . . . He gave Himself.

We have the ability to take responsibility for our own misguided actions. We can humbly ask for forgiveness for those foolish choices and turn from them. Rather than blame God, we have the privilege to honor Him with our choices.

JOURNAL

Define responsibility.

_____
_____
_____
_____

How can you put this responsibility into action in your own life?

_____
_____
_____
_____
_____
_____

What is your heart whispering?

_____
_____
_____
_____
_____
_____
_____
_____
_____
_____
_____
_____
_____
_____
_____
_____
_____

TENACIOUS FAITH

Psalm 115:1
Not to us, O LORD, not to us, but to Your name give glory because of Your lovingkindness {unfailing love*}, because of Your truth.

How is it we doubt, even for a second, what God has spoken into our spirit? Why do we question the giftings, talents, and plans He has placed deep within us?

Perhaps it is the clamoring doubts of others who call us foolish. Or could it be our own insecurities? How about lies from the enemy who hates us and desperately wants us to renounce our faith in our glorious God?

Whatever the reason for our doubt and unbelief, it is imperative we remain strong and stand firm in what we know to be God's truth. While listening to a pastor this morning, his encouragement to have **tenacious faith caused me to liberate myself from several doubts that have crept in.

We, as fellow believers, are to encourage one another to be persistent, stand strong, don't back down, speak out what we know and what we believe. This tenacious challenge is for myself as well.

*New Living Translation
Webster's Online Dictionary
**tenacious - persistent in maintaining, adhering to, or seeking something valued or desired ~
continuing despite difficulties, opposition, or discouragement

JOURNAL

Are you doubting God's plan for you?

_____
_____
_____
_____

What will you do to overcome your doubt?

_____
_____
_____
_____
_____
_____
_____
_____

What is your heart whispering?

_____
_____
_____
_____
_____
_____
_____
_____
_____
_____
_____
_____
_____
_____
_____
_____
_____
_____
_____
_____
_____

TITLE DEED

Hebrews 11:1 AMP
*Now faith is the assurance (title deed, confirmation) of things
hoped for (divinely guaranteed), and the evidence of things
not seen [the conviction of their reality—faith comprehends
as fact what cannot be experienced by the physical senses].*

Title deed. If you ever receive the title deed to your home, you will see your name written in bold caps across the page. This document is saying the price of the property has been paid in full, it belongs to you. It is no longer under the control of the bank or loan company.

Our faith in the work of Jesus Christ on the cross and His miraculous resurrection from death has put His name in bold caps on the title deed of our life. He has paid in full the debt we owed God for every sin we've ever committed or ever will commit.

Just as with a home mortgage, many of us could not imagine paying off the immense debt of our sins in our lifetime. Jesus, however, has accomplished the unimaginable in the spiritual realm. Paying for our sin and overcoming death.

This title deed does not demand bondage or slavery as the debt did. No, it is a gift of freedom for us to look forward to the divine promises we are guaranteed to receive. We may not experience them all right now, but they are definitely real. And because we belong to Jesus and have faith that He lives, those promises are fully ours.

Oh yeah . . .
OUR SAVIOR IS RISEN INDEED

JOURNAL

Define debt.

Define title deed.

What does Jesus' work on the cross mean to you?

What is your heart whispering?

Dear Reader,

In conclusion, I trust you have been blessed by your commitment to devote yourself to 30 days spending time with God.

Now that you have completed this journal, please take time to peruse it and review your journal responses. I have provided an additional journal page for you to ponder how this process has deepened your personal relationship with Him. Celebrate the answered prayers, the insights He has given you, the joy of sharing the whispers of your heart with Him.

I encourage you to continue your commitment by spending time each day with God. Invite Him to enter into your past, clarify your present, and assure you of an eternally joyful future.

JOURNAL

ABOUT THE AUTHOR

Whispers of the Heart, the sixth book in the expanding collection of author Anne Watson's writings, not only gives credence to Anne's calling to 'Get God's word in their hands through her writing' but in this 30 day devotional journal Anne also shares a bit of her own life experiences. For years Anne has poured out her adventures, frustrations, pain and joy in journal form allowing her thoughts and dreams to flow from her heart, through her pen, to God. Anne enjoys engaging with her readers through her website, via email and through her weekly online devotion, *Coffee with God*. Anne makes her home in the lush green beauty of East Texas.

www.AnneWatsonAuthor.com
watsononline1711@gmail.com

OTHER DEVOTIONALS BY ANNE WATSON

HE IS OUR HOPE
A Daily Devotional

Ever felt like the lone poppy on the front cover? Isolated. Vulnerable. Abandoned. Survivor. What we want is . . . Interaction. Vigor. Acceptance. Significance. In our world shrouded in a devastating past, uncontrollable present and an insecure future where can we possibly find hope? Two Words—Jesus Christ.

HE IS OUR KING
A Daily Devotional

A king is known best by the people he rules. But not so with our King, who knows us best. Our King is a perfect king. Lovingly ruling His kingdom. We follow Him who leads us as the Shepherd. But in all things He is our King in the kingdom that has no end.

OTHER WRITINGS BY ANNE WATSON

Jacob's Bend Series Book One
Broken Acres

In a matter of seconds … reality changes everything. At the age of forty-two, with her children scattered in three different states, Madison Crane knows exactly what her future holds. That is until her husband, Jeff, unexpectedly dies.

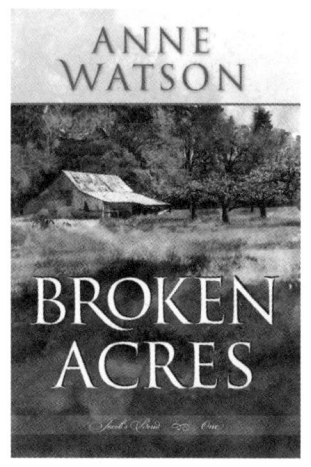

Jacob's Bend Series Book Two
Splintered Lives

When Maddie's dream to make her farm, Broken Acres, a refuge for hurting people becomes a nightmare, she questions what she believes gives her safe haven. Financial security. Land possession. Comfortable cottage. Family. Where is her family when she desperately needs them?

Jacob's Bend Series Book Three
Welcome Home

Welcome to a place called Broken Acres. After almost losing her farm to a devious businessman, Maddie sees a chance to win it back and finally have the opportunity to open it up to those who are hurting. Maddie realizes her dream requires more than a comfortable cottage and a big house for hurting residents to heal.

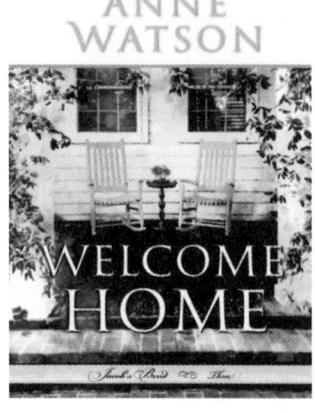